UNSUNG HERO# FREE INDIA MOVEMENT

SH. HARI SEVAK SINGH

SAAVI MANGLA

I dedicate this little book to Late Sh. Hari Sevak Singh Ji

on his

100th Birth Anniversary on 23rd June 2022.

He will always stay alive in our memories and our heart

for

his bravery

and

zeal

to serve the nation and his contribution to India's independence.

Contents

FOREWORD

I am one of the grandsons of Late Sh. Hari Sevak Singh. His life story always inspired me and my family members. So, when Saavi approached me to share his life story to pen down to bring his contribution to the freedom struggle to the world, so that, all would come to know about unsung heroes of the freedom movement. I got agreed immediately and shared whatever I knew.

It was indeed a proud moment for me. Moreover, Saavi has shaped his story wonderfully. It brought tears to my eyes. I am very happy to see this work and waiting for it to get published.

My best wishes are with Saavi.

Sh. Sampurnanand Singh

PREFACE

The 21st century we are in has given us ample Independence. We have enumerated various rights to relish the lives of Indian citizens.

But have we ever thought of fulfilling our Fundamental Duties as a citizen? Rarely do we.

However, this is indeed the result of many unsung heroes that we have got to live with Freedom. Readers, let us embark on the journey of one such unsung hero, Sh Harisevak Ji.

Hari valued freedom and considered it as a moral duty of the citizens to serve the nation. It had always been his earnest desire to get at least one of his family members enrolled in the Army from each generation. His family too has been valuing the tradition set by Hari. From then on, one child has been enrolled in the army.

On this journey, we will be accompanied by Zoya, Aman, and Bara.

Happy Reading.

Acknowledgements

I am thankful to Sh. Sampurnanand Singh,
grandson of Sh Harisevak Ji,
to provide insights and information about the
inspiring life of Harisevak Ji
to pen down the motivating story of his life.

I

Travel in History# India under British Rule

As Zoya, a student of class 8, flipped through the illustrations of her Social studies‘ book boredom spread on her face, amazement overtook her emotions as she felt that the image of a district named 'Barabanki‘ jumped and waved at her.

She shook her head and cleaned her spectacles, and told, “Read more fantasy tales and one day you will surely turn mad”. It was lunchtime, she and her best friend Aman quarrelled over lending the books. Suddenly they were awestruck as the image was successful in her attempt to bulge out of the book.

Aman being a Harry Potter fan waved at the image and a warm welcoming gesture spread over his face. While Zoya was still in shock.

The image introduced herself and said, "Hey!! How are you, buddies? Well, I am Barabunki, you can call me Bara. Okay, wait, why introduce like this...wait I will get a 'Timecopter', so just wear it and adjust this 'Timometer' to visit the place you want to visit...TIME TRAVEL" hearing this, a long quarrel begun between the two besties, one wanted to visit the Mughal era, while the other wanted to visit the Mahabharata times to know if it existed.

However, amidst this quarrel, the 'Timecopter' got automatically activated and miraculously they found themselves flying in the sky of the image. Suddenly with a thud, they landed on the veranda of a haveli. They were awestruck by the architectural difference. They pinched each other to check if it's real.

On realising it's true, they walked around the haveli and looked at each of the painting. Now they could relate to their history lessons. Suddenly they saw two men approaching, they hid behind the pillar, but Bara came and said, "Oh dear don't worry no one can see u both. But remember not to touch or eat anything. Well, I have got these yummy snacks... you can have them on your journey." Zoya and Aman walked freely around the haveli, suddenly they heard the sounds of the cry of a baby.

Well, who was this child? Let us explore this, and turn the pages.

II

Zamindaari System# Forced Lagaan

Let us connect the thread to where we left in the previous chapter. We were in the year 1922 where the child crying was named to be Harisevak Singh. His mother called him with affection 'Hari'.

Hari was born in the Barabanki District of Uttar Pradesh. He was an adorable but notorious child. Being one of the three sons of a renowned Landlord, he was blessed born with a silver spoon.

The country was under British rule and was suffering from the Political tactics of these undesirable guests. However, Hari's childhood was being passed in all the comforts of life, away from the cruelty of time that was meted upon the poorer sections of society.

Aman, being quite weak in history wondered, "what job was Hari's father supposed to do?"

Zoya answered "You don't remember the zamindari system? Well, I have read in one of the books in the Library. Under this system Colonials used to appointed zamindars who were supposed to collect 'Lagaan' from the farmers. A portion of whatever they can accumulate from the poor peasants goes to the Britishers and the remaining portion belongs to the zamindars.

The zamindars some time out of greed or other times because of helplessness use various tactics to gather as much revenue from the tillers as possible. That creates an environment of torture and suppression."

Aman exclaimed, "Now I got it. Thank you, well indeed you will be a great historian!".

Time passed. The toddler Hari is promoted to class 4th. You must be wondering that he must be satisfied and joyous by the British rule. Well, no... not at all. Hari clearly understood the job his father was performing for the Britishers. He rather always remained worn out towards his father. He firmly stood up against his father and encouraged him to give up such a cruel job.

His eyes continuously nurturing the dream of taking part in the Indian Freedom Struggle.

However, every time he expressed his desire, his father rebuked, "All these luxuries you are experiencing and enjoying are all gifts of Britisher." But all days are not red as roses.

One day, his father experienced the death of a neighbour due to the lack of hospital in the village, he got very disappointed. He immediately presented before the magistrate his proposal to set up schools and hospitals in the Barabanki village. But, what could one expect from the shrewd exploitation? They straightaway rejected the proposal because the funds were not sufficient. Zamindar

Sahab knew very well that the money deposited with the Britishers for the quarter was more than enough for such establishments. On this betrayal of Britishers, zamindar Sahab was shocked.

He headed back towards his home. His mind got flooded with many thought. Devastated, he moved ahead.

He promised, “I would never restrict Hari from taking a stand against the colonials. One day he would join the Freedom Struggle.”

III

Lack of Education# Joined British Army

The years rolled by, now Hari was a grown-up boy of 18 yr but he could complete his studies till class 4. In spite of his struggles to study ahead, he couldn't because of British policies. Britishers did not provide higher education to Indians so that they can rule comfortably without many obstacles. but Hari's zeal to do something fruitful for the motherland did not fade away. However, the speed of this car of Nationalism got ultimately fueled by the support of Hari's father.

Though he continued as a zamindar, he secretly developed discontentment towards the shrewd colonial rulers. Thus this father-son duo was on a secret mission to one day oust these Britishers out of their own home; their motherland.

Hari believed that the day when these exploiters will be thrown out of their land will be the day when the flowers, birds, animals and humans will be able to lead a free life. The road to their aim was hazed by the clouds.

One such day as he and his friend...Oh!! I forgot to introduce to you all one of the main characters of this story!! It's indeed none other than Shiv Prasad, Hari Sewak Ji's best buddy. They were childhood friends who shared an incredible bond. They were each other's secret box. So today, as they were strolling through the market, they encountered that the Britishers were recruiting men for armed forces in the 2nd world war. There was a situation of chaos in the market, they were just capturing all above 18 yr and forcing them to join the British Army.

Hari and Shiv were eager to grab the opportunity as they lured them to Free India, if they join. A huge storm was awaiting as Hari's family strongly opposed his decision. Zamindar babu was fierce on hearing his decision. He believes that this was not at all the way he could serve the nation. However, Hari's decision was too strong to be changed. Hence, he eloped from the house with Shiv to join the British armed forces in 1938.

Hari felt that his dream will come true, unaware of the fact that many more challenges and twists were awaiting ahead. In the British army, they were given rigorous training. Initially, everything seemed to be like a dream come true as he viewed himself as a fighter, however, as it is said not every shiny thing is gold. Similar was the scenario of this British army system.

The soldiers recruited were trained in a camp set up by the colonials. Hari and Shiv were pleased on entering the Camp. The British army was like a beautifully wrapped gift for the Indians, whom they used as mere puppets to maintain their rule in the colony. Gradually this gift was unwrapped by Shiv and Hari both were dismayed on finding the true side of the coin. Though the salary provided was lucrative, but was nothing more than a rattrap.

The soldiers were consistently disrespected and discriminated against on the grounds of their nationality. The promotion system was a huge issue. The problem was similar to what we face today in the corporate world i. e. like a glass ceiling. Only the officers from England were subject to be promoted to a high level. Indians were mere dust for them and considered deserving only lower posts. Hari and Shiv were bound to follow the rules which were against their free will.

But something more intriguing was awaiting ahead.

IV

Dual British Policies # Discrimination

As days passed, the reality of the British army was unveiled. Hari gradually realised why his father opposed his decision. This realisation was struck owing to the series of acts witnessed by Hari and Shiv.

One day, as the two along with their squad members were proceeding to have lunch, they heard a loud shout. On reaching the spot, they saw one of the members from the other squad was being punished as he was asking for the dish that was meant for the British soldiers. This left Hari baffled.

Later on that day, he overheard the conversation between the chief and a British soldier, they decided to reduce the salary and food consumption of the Indian Soldiers. This did not come as a big shock to Hari as he knew the ideology of the Britishers.

One incident turned the table around, on one of their field trips, the team got stuck in between a tribal forest. The tribals on seeing the British uniforms, initiated the fight and during fighting with some tribals, one of the Indian Soldiers got injured while saving the life of a British soldier, This too did not melt the hearts of Britishers, and they refused to provide any aid to the injured soldier, as there was only one doctor available that too a British doctor. There was a division of even medical facilities.

The superior quality service and priority were given to the British officials. The Indians were expected to be sidelined. Even after requests, the British refused to send medical aid.

At that time, Hari and Shiv gathered all their courage and paved the way for their team's rescue.

V

Life changing step # Azad Hind Fauz

This incident with tribals left Hari awestruck. He was disturbed. It left him with a realization, that his aim to serve his motherland was slipping out of his hands like the sand.

In his dreams, he heard the injured Indian soldier scream. He realized that they were just being exploited in the name of fighting for the nation. This realization filled him with the guilt of going against his father's word. Later, when he shared his thoughts with Shiv, he instinctively told that this is quite normal, and "We have to adjust".

On seeing no other way, Hari too agreed to it. Soon in around 1941, the news of Subhash Chandra Bose forming INA(Indian National Army or Azad Hind Fauz) started being muffled in ears. As soon as it reached Hari's ears, he was filled with excitement as his long-lost desire of becoming the Freedom Fighter, was taking the right shape now.

He shared his excitement with Shiv. Shiv too expressed his happiness, however, a moment later, he said, "I have heard, the salary and perks are lower as compared to what we get now, by serving the British army. I don't want to leave such a high salary!" Shiv's statement left a rift between the two besties. They landed up in an argument that lasted along. However, Shiv after a lot of contemplation understood Hari's point of view and fulfilled the promise that both of them made to each other, not to leave each other's hand even in the darkest of the days.

Hence these two warriors secretly telegrammed the INA recruiters for their selection. The day they received the secret message of their selection, their joy was unmeasurable. The days for the INA Camp were nearing Shiv and Hari increased their practice regime. They gathered all their equipment and filed for their resignation. Though not willing, due to the pressure and agony Of these two soldiers, Britishers had to bend and give a stamp on their resignation.

However, more hurdles were waiting at the door of Hari and Shiv.

VI

Life at INA # Full of challenges

Resigning British Army was indeed not the end of Hari and Shiv's journey, it was just a mere stoppage. A large part of the journey was yet to be travelled. A life full of dreams and a spirit to achieve their dream was waiting for them. At INA. they underwent a rigorous exercise at the camp. During the exercises, they were taught how to fight the opponent even with minimum equipment. The job was even tougher as the equipment with INA were less advanced as compared to the British Army, thus increasing the risk to their lives.

All of them were very well aware of these consequences before joining INA. Hari's hard work and dedication to serving the nation was incomparable. Time fled by and stars conspired to lead this story of Independence full of "conflict".

On seeing Hari's dedication, one day, Commandant said, "Hari it is great to see your hard work and logic with which you tackle the situations. Seeing your capabilities, with huge expectations, I give you the responsibility of leading the army contingent heading towards Burma for the World War."

Hari was elated to know this, he was getting alert as danger was approaching and situations grew difficult. He was determined to get his contingent fully ready for the worst of the situations. To achieve that, the first milestone was to make the soldiers understand the meaning of team spirit. To make them realise the same, Hari and Shiva together resorted to experimenting.

The soldiers were asked to go on a forest visit and as per the plan, they were trapped inside a den. Though all the essentials were available inside the den trap. The need was... only a united step... to discover them. Elsewhere, after playing a lot of blame games, the members realised that it was all in vain to quarrel amongst themselves. They analysed each other's strengths and used various logic to survive.

Few members were started struggling to open the den, while some other searched for food, others strived to light the fire to assist with lighting and making the environment warmer to resist the freezing weather in the den.

It was a memorable moment as those people who earlier fought like Tom and Jerry were now seen helping each other to get through the situation. Everyone shared the burden and in this course realised that indeed, if, they stood united, the toughest of situations became easier.

On their successful accomplishment of coming out of the den, a change was evident in their bonds and behaviour. The days saw improvement in the performance of the soldiers.

One day, a spy arrived and informed something to Hari. To which he looked baffled.

What was it ....it is a mystery to be unveiled in further chapters. Yes...another challenge is waiting for him.

VII

Burma movement # Step towards freedom

The spy informed Hari of the coming storm. Indeed, they had been preparing for such storms but still, a slight wave of confused feeling touched him but on seeing the courage and unitedness of the soldiers, he jerked out the baffling feelings and gathered courage within himself to face the worst situation.

His strength was the 'sparkling eyes of his father' when he joined INA. He marched ahead and motivated his soldiers to buckle up themselves to fight for what they all joined Azad Hind Fauj.

He said "Saathiyo! Now is the time to make the aim of this army a reality. Now is the time that we give ourselves to let our country breathe free air. Now is the time that we make our country "Aazad" from the shackles of foreigners. Second World War has been initiated and after a lot of strategic planning, Mr bose has succeeded in finding our allies against the foreigners. Burma has promised to support the struggle for freedom. The ball is in our court to show the courage and loyalty towards the nation."

On hearing all this, the soldiers shouted "Jai Hind"; the energy and strategy of the team were set. They all marched towards Burma, their ultimate destination. Varied geographical conditions were to be crossed to reach the destination, a lot of investigation about the varied landforms and the climatic conditions was already done. Food and other essentials were safely packed to ensure no shortage. The duties like cooking food, guarding at night the lamppost, medical aids etc were distributed.

The journey was tough as many soldiers got injured but their courage was not lowered. The doctor and nurse dedicatedly served the soldiers to ensure their safe arrival in Burma. Finally, after a long travel Burma was there. Settlements were made in such a place, with similar coloured clothing, so that no one could recognise them easily.

At night a sudden outbreak of firing baffled them, but they managed to face the enemies. Shiv got injured. Blood was flowing out from his left arm. Doctors said, "Mr Hari, Shiv is in a critical situation, but still, we need a blood group and blood donor. Hari did everything to save his childhood friend. His state grew worse as hours passes, but finally, the doctor said something that gave relief to everyone. Shiv's condition started improving and he was out of danger. Hari took a sigh of relief.

Both smiled and come out more strong and determined to achieve their life's goal.

VIII

Azad Hind Fauj # Dream come true

The journey was not a bed of roses. The circumstances of the world were not in favour of mankind. The darkened windows of houses and silent streets showed that indeed India was in turmoil.

The double wars being fought on the Indian land gave our motherland pain and relief too as everyone strived hard for her independence. The soldiers silently marched towards their destination with only one aim in their mind "Swaraj" to see the 'Sun after Independence' and breathe the air that is fresh and of "New Bharat."

In World war two, Azad Hind Fauj declines to fight for Britishers and joined hands with Japan. Japan agreed to extend help to INA. As they reached, they were allotted various tents. Now they could practice but without any movement and noise as the environment was not good.

At night sudden bombarding started, though not well prepared, all of them fought the hidden enemies. On hearing the sudden bombarding, the soldiers hastened to reach out to the arsenal. They divided themselves into teams and kept a check on different duties essential to be tracked. One team proceeded towards the arsenal, the other towards the main entrance, few to the lampposts to see the exact location of the enemy, while others marched in different directions.

Those days were not technologically advanced to have a Public Addressing System or even telegraphs. That made the situation graver. The communication gap resulted in a delay in bullet supply. The war was a tough one resulted in the vast devastation caused. But it made us clear that indeed prevention is better than cure. Thus they made themselves ready for more such jerks.

After this incident, it becomes critical for the security of the battalion, to displace to a safer and higher place to easily track the movements taking place. After everyone took a rest, a meeting was held and discussed the possibilities of the new location. After a lot of discussion and brainstorming, finally, the team held on to the "Popa Hills". However, a line of worry appeared on Hari's face.

He shared, "The peak of this hill is muddy and clayey, we might not be able to defend ourselves. The floor is slippery can be quite risky."

To this, Shiv replied worriedly, "Bhai, no other place is suitable for us. This is the nearest and highest place in this region. We can find a solution once we reach there."

Though this decision did not seem to be much appealing, however looking at the prevailing situation, Hari gave his consent and agreed. The soldiers were again set to embark on a further journey.

IX

Nuclear Bomb # Horrifying Bloodshed

The journey to Mount Popa was smooth during the daylight. Despite their planning, it became dark by the time they reached the peak of Mount Popa. Indeed, they faced a hard time.

The place was muddy and clayey; it was just impossible for them to settle their tents. Even the woods were too dense to find some space. It was a tough time for the battalion. However, they managed with the cooked food that had been left uneaten in the morning. Though it was not sufficient, they shared amongst themselves to sustain till the next ray of sunlight.

The temperature of the night sky made their sustenance even more challenging. They decided to exercise to adjust the body temperature with the environment. It helped and reduced their misery to some extent. However, in the deepest corner of their hearts, each of them prayed, "God please no more attacks for at least tonight."

But then a soldier's duty and inner voice dejected it and urged, "You are a warrior, you have to fight whatever may come. Don't act like a coward." No one had any clue what will come next.

This night God appeared to have blessed them all on seeing the courage and strength with which they strived to perform their duty to the best of their potential. The soldiers slept peacefully, unknown of the awaiting storm ahead.

The next morning, Sun bring along a spy who came running to the peak. On seeing his expression, Hari understood the gravity of the situation. However, at 4 AM war commenced again, though the sun was yet not rising. They again arranged themselves. Captain Khan heroically fought but got injured while saving Sipahi Shyam. The INA gradually paved its way to the deepest of the enemy's den. However, as it appeared that everything was alright, something unexpected happened. Spy Raju came rushing and said "Captain, Bomb....Bomb...Nuclear Bomb on Hiroshima, Nagasaki....tabahi ...tabahi much Gayi hai..., Japan lost to Britain....Surrender karna padega...." Hari got shocked and become thoughtful, " Surrender....? When we are on the verge of victory....when we are on the verge to defeat Brisitish Army...We are bound to surrender... Oh God..."

It came as a shock for all of them. As the army surrendered, though disheartened, they hugged each other and appreciated the bravery they showed throughout the journey till now. Many soldiers were injured and many had been brought to death by these injured soldiers. While many happily sacrificed their lives for the bright Sun of

Independent India.

X

Big Blow # Surrender before British Army

All the soldiers were made to surrender. They were imprisoned but the zeal to see the bright independent sun in India did not get obscured. The zeal was intact even after the tortures meted upon them in the prison. However, the incapability of reaching out to loved ones always gripped them. Those times were not as easy as present in India.

Unlike today, they didn't have the facility of getting connected just by clicking a link to the meet. I wonder, if this would have been possible in those days, the life would have been eased, the struggle would have been minimized. Then the pain of separation and being imprisoned in a foreign land would not have been so hurting. They were caged in the prison from 1943-1947. Indeed, those years had been heart-wrecking. The sole medium of communication prevalent at that time was mailing letters. However, those letters too reached after the deadlinc had crossed.

Hari was tormented by the pain of separation and thoughts troubled him. He impatiently waited for the time when he and Shiv would return to their hometown. To decrease the ache of the heart, they drenched themselves in work. They found out works that engage them for more time. They carried the stone bag on back, sometimes baked the bricks, some saw them sweeping the darkest floor and transforming it to the whitest.

The time rolled by and the news of "Indian Independence" blew in the air. This news reached Hari and Shiv's ears too. They were delighted to know this. To celebrate this, they saved the sweet served in lunch for the dinner! At night, they together ate the sweet and relived their childhood memories. Sitting in the jail, they laughed at silly fights they used to do and time spent with the family. They dreamt of meeting their families after a long time. Few days passed, and the day of their final release came. They left the prison with full enthusiasm. However, Hari was not aware of the impending changes he was going to face.

XI

New Begining # Ray of Hope

On reaching Barabanki, they were astonished by various developments. As they walked to their houses, they realized that many neighbors had been displaced owing to the Partition. This pained them. However, this was nothing before what destiny had decided for Hari.

On his arrival at Haveli, he called out his mother, "Amma" but no one responded. His brothers came and greeted him. However, soon he heard the news for which his ears were not ready. Hari's father and mother had passed. No one informed him as they were not sure of his whereabouts. The land too had been distributed by Bauji amongst other brothers. This was done to preserve the land which could otherwise be taken away by the govt. New land reforms had knocked on the door and bauji found it the best way.

Those times were indeed miserable. However, Hari did not lose hope and started fresh. He joined the Police force as

Company Commander in Homeguards Department. Later on, the distorted family too came together and the brothers settled by giving Hari his rightful share.

Recognition is a must to appraise those who work hard to achieve a collective goal. This brings to their respect and smile on their faces. On one of Mrs. Indira Gandhi's, the then Prime minister of India, visits to England, she realized this. On returning, the first thing she did was to honor those who served INA in the Indian struggle for Freedom. The invaluable contribution of those soldiers was finally recognized in the year 1975. The government initiated the Pension Yojana for these brave warriors as well.

Hari valued freedom and considered it as a moral duty of the citizens to serve the nation. It had always been his earnest desire to get at least one of his family members enrolled in the Army from each generation. His family too has been valuing the tradition set by Hari. From then on, one child has been enrolled in the army. For Hari, joining Army was a Pride.

Indeed his successors have understood this and have left no stone unturned to achieve Harisevak ji's dream.

XII

Atamnirbhar Bharat # Dream of Many Unsung Heroes

"Zoya, Aman!! Wake up!!" the classmates shouted to awaken them.

On waking up, they both looked at each other with amazement.

As they went past the corridor, their History teacher, called them and asked " So children, how was your travel...time..?"

This struck them with surprise and asked.... "which travel mam?"

Mam said, "I hope it had been an interesting journey and you learned a lot of things on your journey."

She smiled at both of them and went away.

They both said, “Now I see .... It had been so much struggle to get to India that we see and live in today.”

Aman said, "Indeed our History has so many mysteries and stories still undiscovered. Zoya....once you become Historian....pl share your researches with me so that I can get to know more about our past."

"Ok”, Zoya replied. They both laughed and boarded their bus.

Zoya said, “HARI was so brave....The soldiers strived to achieve their goals. We must also be determined to build the bright future of India.”

Aman said, "You are right...sometimes by chance, you say the right things as well!”

Both of them quarreled and giggled to get set go on a new journey that awaited them in the Future.

In the school’s assembly area, ‘Tiranga’ was swirling with pride in the gentle breeze.

PHOTO GALLERY HARISEVAK JI AND HIS FAMILY

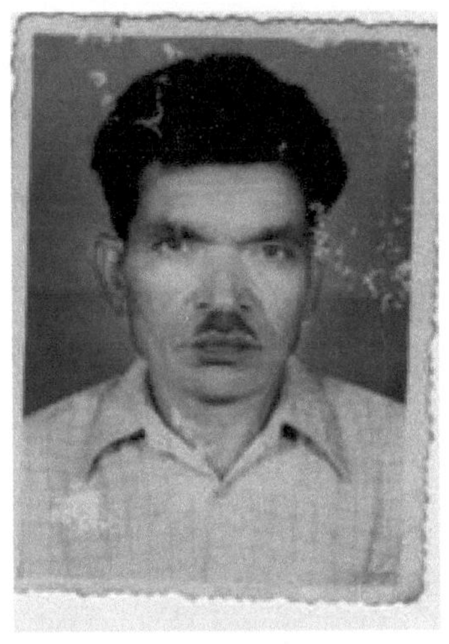

Harisevak ji

At his village

An example of 'Simple Living High Thinking'

A simple hero

स्व.श्री हरिसेवक सिंह
रामानंद सिंह
स्वतन्त्रता संग्राम सेनानी "आजाद हिन्द फौज"

About The Writer

Saavi Mangla

Saavi is a young writer pursuing a Bachelor of Business Administration from Nirma University Ahmedabad and preparing for Chartered Accountancy. She is a passionate person and loves to write. She has been an avid writer and has written blogs for various Non-Profit Organisations.

Her story 'NAZRANA' got third 'Narayani Puruskar' from Book Trust of India and was published by the trust. She has also contributed three articles for an anthology, "Deep Thinking for Thinkers", published by Rosewood Publications.

Besides her passion for writing, she is an artist and a debater as well.

"Jai Hind Jai Bharat"

Printed by Libri Plureos GmbH in Hamburg,
Germany